MW00512786

THE BREAD MAKING COOKBOOK

A Home Baker's Journey in 50 Recipes

Alfredo Toscana

Table of Contents

Baked Cheddar Toast

Categories: Breads, Cheese, Eggs, Main dish

Servings: 6

Ingredient

- ❖ 1 c Heavy Or Whipping Cream
- ❖ 1 c Cheddar Cheese; Md, Shredded
- ❖ 1/2 ts Nutmeg 1/4 ts White Pepper
- ❖ 4 Eggs; Lg, Well Beaten 12 Bread Slices; White

Preparation

On top of a double boiler, combine cream, cheddar, white pepper, and nutmeg.

Stir over hot water until the cheese melts and the mixture is well blended.

Remove from the heat and cool to lukewarm. Generously butter a large baking sheet and set aside.

Cut bread slices diagonally and dip each triangle into your cheddar mixture.

Place 1/2-inch apart on baking sheet and bake until browned and bubbly, about 15 minutes. Serve hot.

French Toast Cheddar Sandwiches

Categories: Breads, Cheese, Eggs, Main dish, Sandwiches

Servings: 4

Ingredient

- ❖ 2 Eggs; Lg 1/3 c Milk or Light Cream
- ❖ 1/2 ts Salt 8 White Bread; Slices
- ❖ Mustard; Prepared 4 Cheddar Cheese; Thick,Slices
- ❖ 3 tb Butter

Preparation

Set out a heavy skillet or cast-iron griddle. Beat eggs slightly in a pie tin or shallow bowl and add the milk or cream and salt, set aside.

Spread the bread slices out on a flat working surface. Spread one side of four slices of bread lightly with the prepared mustard.

Top each with a slice of cheddar cheese. Butter the remaining four slices of bread and top each cheese slice with bread, butter side down. Heat the butter in the skillet or on the griddle.

Carefully dip each sandwich into egg mixture, coating both sides. Allow the excess egg mixture to drain back into the bowl.

Dip only as many sandwiches as will lie flat in the skillet or griddle.

Cook over low heat until browned. Turn and brown the other side. Repeat for the remaining sandwiches and if necessary, add more butter to the skillet or griddle to prevent sticking.

Or you can place the sandwiches, after dipping, on a well-greased baking sheet and brown in the oven at 450 degrees F. for 8 to 10 minutes. Serve hot.

Stuffed Rolls

Categories: Breads, Cheese, Main dish, Sandwiches, Vegetables

Servings: 6

Ingredient

- ❖ 16 oz Cheddar; Sharp, shredded 8 oz Green Olives; Stuffed*
- ❖ 2 Green Bell Peppers; Md 12 French Rolls; Large
- ❖ 6 oz Tomato Sauce; * 1 Onion; Md.

* These are approximate sizes. Recipe called for 1 small jar of stuffed olives and 1 can of tomato sauce. It should be to your taste.

Preparation

Cut the tops off the rolls and hollow them out leaving a thin shell.

Grind all ingredients and bread in a meat grinder or food processor and stuff back into the rolls.

Place the tops back on the rolls and secure with toothpicks.

Bake on an ungreased cookie sheet at 350 degrees F. For about 45 minutes. Serve Hot.

Poppin' Fresh Barbe Cups

Categories: Breads, Cheese, Main dish, Meats, Sandwiches

Servings: 6

Ingredient

- ❖ 3/4 lb Ground Beef; Lean 1 tb Onion; Minced
- ❖ 2 tb Brown Sugar 12 Biscuits; *
- ❖ 1/2 c Barbecue Sauce; ** 3/4 c Cheddar; Sharp, Shredded

* Use 1 8-oz tube of store-bought biscuits, or your favourite 12 biscuit recipe. ** Use store bought sauce or your favourite recipe

Preparation

In a skillet brown the ground beef and then drain off the excess fat Add the BBQ sauce, onion and brown sugar and set aside.

Separate the biscuit dough into 12 pieces and place one in each of 12 ungreased muffin cups, pressing the dough up the sides to edge of the cup.

Spoon the mixture into the cups and sprinkle with the shredded Cheddar Cheese.

Bake in a preheated 400 degrees F. oven for 12 minutes. Serve hot

VARIATIONS:

Use one 13-oz can of chili beans in place of the meat mixture (or 1 13-oz can of baked beans, and frankfurters or hot dogs that have been cut into pieces) in place of the meat mixture.

You can also add green bell pepper or a hot pepper to the above recipe with good results.

Cheddar Crackers

Categories: Breads, Crackers, Cheese

Servings: 6

Ingredient

- ❖ 1/2 c Butter Or Margarine 1 1/2 c Unbleached Flour; Sifte
- ❖ 1/2 ts Salt 1 ts Baking Powder
- ❖ 1 ds Cayenne Pepper 2 c Cheddar; Extra Sharp*

* The Extra Sharp Cheddar Cheese should be finely grated.

Preparation

Stir dry ingredients into a bowl and then cut in butter to resembl cornmeal. Blend in cheddar cheese with a fork until well blended.

Mix in remaining ingredients and shape into 1 1/2 to 2-inch rolls.

Chill for 30 to 40 minutes in the refrigerator and then slice each ro into slices about 1/4-inch thick. Bake on an ungreased cookie shee at 400 degrees F for about 10 minutes. Remove from cookie shee and let cool.

Store the cooled crackers in airtight containers in a cool place. The will keep for several weeks this way and if you freeze them, the will last indefinitely.

Cheddar-Olive Bread

Categories: Breads, Cheese, Vegetables

Servings: 6

Ingredient

- ❖ 3 c Cheddar; Sharp, grated 3 oz Pimento stuffed olives; sliced
- ❖ 1 c Mayonnaise 1 French Bread; Loaf, Unsliced

Preparation

Mix the cheese, olives, and mayonnaise together.

Spread on the cut surface of French Bread, which has been sliced horizontally.

Bake at 350 degrees F for 20 to 30 minutes, then slice into thick slices and serve hot.

Chili-Cheese Bread

Categories: Breads, Vegetables

Servings: 6

Ingredient

- ❖ 3 c Monterey Jack Cheese; Grated 4 oz Chiles; Chopped, *
- ❖ 1 c Mayonnaise 1 French Bread; Loaf, Unsliced

* You can use one can of sweet green chiles or jalapenos that have been chopped.

Preparation

Mix the cheese, peppers, and mayonnaise, blending well.

Spread on cut surface of the French bread, which has been sliced in half horizontally.

Bake at 350 degrees F for 20 to 30 minutes and cut into thick slices and serve hot.

Cheddar Fans

Categories: Breads, Cheese, Quickbreads

Servings: 4

Ingredient

- ❖ 5 oz Cheddar; Sharp, grated 2 c Unbleached Flour; Sifted
- ❖ 1 tb Baking Powder 1 ts Salt
- ❖ 1/2 c Butter or Shortening 1/2 c Milk
- ❖ Butter; Softened Butter; Melted

Preparation

Grease the bottoms of 12 muffin pan cups. Grate the cheese into a bowl, if not already grated and set aside.

Sift the flour, baking powder and salt into a bowl.

Cut in the shortening with a pastry blender or two knives, until the mixture resembles coarse corn meal.

Make a well in the centre of mixture and add the milk all at once.

Stir with a fork until the dough forms a ball. Gently form the dough into a ball and put on a lightly floured surface.

Knead it lightly with the fingertips 10 or 15 times.

Roll the dough into a 12 X 10-inch rectangle about 1/4-inch thick.

Cut into 5 strips and spread with the softened butter.

Sprinkle four strips with grated cheddar cheese and stack four on top of one another and top with the fifth strip.

Cut into 12 equal pieces and place on end in the muffin cups.

Brush the tops of rolls with the melted butter.

Bake at 450 degrees F. for 10 to 15 minutes or until the biscuits are golden brown.

Serve hot with butter. Makes 1 dozen Cheddar Fans.

Little Cheddar Biscuits

Categories: Breads, Cheese, Quickbreads

Servings: 8

Ingredient

- ❖ 2 c Unbleached Flour 1 ts Mustard; Dry
- ❖ 1 ts Paprika 1/4 ts Baking Powder
- ❖ 1 c Butter; Room Temperature 10 oz Cheddar; Sharp, grated
- ❖ 1 ts Worcestershire Sauce

Preparation

Combine flour, dry mustard, paprika, baking powder in a medium bowl.

Beat the butter, either by hand or with an electric mixer at medium speed, until light and fluffy.

Slowly beat in the cheddar cheese and Worcestershire sauce.

Gradually add flour mixture, stirring with a fork, until well blended

On a lightly floured surface, shape the dough into a long roll about 1 3/4-inches in diameter.

Wrap in plastic wrap or foil. Place on a platter and refrigerate for at least 2 hours, better overnight.

Preheat the oven to 325 degrees F. Slice the dough about 1/3 inch thick. With your hands, roll each slice into a ball.

Flatten slightly and place on an ungreased baking sheet about two inches apart.

Bake 8 minutes in the preheated oven. Biscuits will only brown slightly on the bottom.

Cheddar Biscuits

Categories: Breads, Cheese, Quickbreads

Servings: 8

Ingredient

- ❖ 2 c Unbleached Flour; Sifted 4 ts Baking Powder
- ❖ 1/2 ts Salt 1 c Cheddar; Sharp, Grated
- ❖ 1/4 c Butter 2/3 c Milk

Preparation

Sift the flour, baking powder, and salt together and mix with grated cheddar cheese.

Cut the butter into the dry ingredients, add the milk and mix quickly but thoroughly.

Dough should be soft. Turn onto a floured board and knead lightly for a few seconds.

Pat to a 3/8-inch thickness and cut. Bake on a baking sheet in a hot oven (450 degrees F.) about 30 minutes or until lightly browned. Serve hot.

Cheddar Pinwheels

Categories: Breads, Cheese, Quickbreads

Servings: 6

Ingredient

- ❖ 2 c Unbleached Flour; Sifted 1/2 ts Salt

- ❖ 1 tb Baking Powder 1/4 c Butter

- ❖ 2/3 c Milk 1 c Cheddar; Extra Sharp, Grated

Preparation

Sift flour, salt, and baking powder together in a mixing bowl, the cut into the butter.

Add the milk and stir together quickly but thoroughly. Turn out on a floured board and knead for 30 seconds then roll out to a 1/8-inch thickness.

Spread with the grated cheese and roll up tightly like cinnamon rolls.

Cut into 3/4-inch slices and transfer to baking sheets and bake in a moderate oven (375 degrees F.) for 20 minutes or until delicately browned.

Cheddar Bread Ring

Categories: Cheese, Breads, Yeast bread

Servings: 4

Ingredient

- ❖ 2 3/4 c Bread Flour 2 tb Sugar; Granulated
- ❖ 1 pk Active Dry Yeast; OR 1 tb Active Dry Yeast; Bulk
- ❖ 3/4 ts Salt 1 c Milk
- ❖ 2 tb Butter 1 1/2 c Cheddar; Sharp, Shredded Butter

NOTE: You can use Unbleached All-Purpose flour in this recipe and up to 3 cups total.

Preparation

Combine 1 1/2 cups of the flour, the sugar, undissolved yeast, and salt thoroughly in a large bowl. Heat the milk and butter together until very warm (115-125 degrees F.).

Gradually add to the dry ingredients and beat at medium speed on an electric mixer for 2 minutes, scraping the bowl occasionally.

Add 1/2 cup of the flour and the cheese. Beat fir 2 minutes on high speed on the mixer, scraping the bowl occasionally.

Stir in enough additional flour to make a stiff but light dough. Turn the dough out onto a lightly floured surface and knead until smooth and elastic, 5 to 8 minutes.

Place in a greased bowl, turning once to grease the top. Cover with a dishtowel that has been soaked in hot water and then wrung out until almost dry.

Let rise in a warm place until doubled in bulk, about 1 hour.

Punch the dough down and turn out on a lightly floured surface and shape into a 20-inch rope.

Place seam side down in a buttered 6 1/2 cup ring mold, pinching the ends together.

Cover and let rise in warm place until nearly doubled in bulk, about 35 to 40 minutes. Bake in a preheated 350-degree F. oven for 25 to 30 minutes. Remove from the ring mold.

NOTE: For a softer crust, brush with melted butter while still hot. Crust will become crisp when cool if you do not.

Golden Spoon Bread

Categories: Breads, Cheese, Quickbreads

Servings: 6

Ingredient

- ❖ 10 oz Cheddar; Sharp, Grated 2 c Milk
- ❖ 4 Egg Yolks; Lg 1 c Corn Meal; Yellow
- ❖ 1/4 c Butter 1 ts Sugar
- ❖ 1/2 ts Salt 4 Egg Whites; Lg

Preparation

Thoroughly grease a 1 1/2-quart casserole dish. Place cheddar in small bowl and set aside. Scald the milk in the top of a double boiler

Meanwhile beat egg yolks until thick and lemon-coloured then set them aside.

When the milk is scalded, add the corn meal very gradually, stirring constantly. Stir until the mixture thickens and becomes smooth.

Remove the top of the double boiler from the simmering water and gradually add the beaten egg yolks, stirring constantly. Mix in grated cheese, butter, sugar and salt. Beat the egg whites, in a small bowl until round peaks are formed.

Gently spread beaten egg whites over the corn meal mixture then carefully fold together until just blended.

Turn the mixture into the greased casserole dish.

Bake at 375 degrees F. for 35 to 40 minutes or until a wooden pick or cake tester comes out clean when inserted in the centre of the dish. Serve piping hot with butter and maple syrup or honey.

Cheddar Dumplings

Categories: Breads, Cheese, Main dish, Quickbreads

Servings: 4

Ingredient

- ❖ 16 oz Cheddar; Md, Shredded 2 Eggs; Lg
- ❖ 1 c Unbleached Flour 1 ts Salt
- ❖ 3 qt Boiling Water 1/2 c Butter
- ❖ 1/2 pt Sour Cream

-------------------------------GARNISHES---------------------------

- ❖ Paprika
- ❖ Parsley

Preparation

Mash the cheddar cheese and add the eggs mixing well.

Stir in flour and salt. Drop by TBLS into rapidly boiling water then cover and boil for 15 minutes.

Drain and serve with melted butter and sour cream.

Sprinkle with chopped parsley or paprika, if desired.

Golden Cheddar Corn Bread

Categories: Breads, Cheese, Side dishes, Quickbreads

Servings: 6

Ingredient

- ❖ 1 c Corn Meal; White If Poss. 1 c Unbleached Flour
- ❖ 1 tb Baking Powder 1 1/2 ts Salt
- ❖ 10 oz Cheddar; Sharp, Shredded 1 c Milk
- ❖ 1/4 c Butter, Melted 1 Egg; Lg, Beaten

Preparation

Combine the dry ingredients and then stir in the cheddar cheese.

Combine the milk, butter and egg then add them to dry ingredients, mixing until just moistened.

Pour into a greased 8-inch square baking pan and bake at 425 degrees F for 35 minutes. Serve hot.

Apple-Cheddar Muffins

Categories: Breads, Cheese, Fruits, Quickbreads

Servings: 4

Ingredient

- ❖ 1/2 c Shortening 1/2 c Sugar; Granulated
- ❖ 2 Eggs; Lg 1 1/2 c Unbleached Flour
- ❖ 1 ts Baking Soda 1 ts Baking Powder
- ❖ 1/2 ts Salt 3/4 c Oats; Quick Cooking
- ❖ 1 c Apples; Finely Chopped 2/3 c Cheddar; Sharp Coarse Grate
- ❖ 1/2 c Pecans; Chopped 3/4 c Milk
- ❖ Apple Slices; * Butter; Melted
- ❖ Cinnamon-Sugar Mixture

* You should have 12 to 15 thin slices of unpeeled red apple for this recipe.

Preparation

Preheat the oven to 400 degrees F. Cream the shortening and sugar together and add eggs, one at a time, beating after each addition.

Combine flour, baking powder, baking soda, and salt in a mixing bowl, mix lightly.

Gradually stir the flour mixture into the shortening mixture. In th order, add oats cheddar and pecans, mixing well after each additio

Gradually add the milk, stirring until all the ingredients are just moistened.

Grease the muffin pans and fill each cup 2/3rds full of batter. Di the apple slices in the melted butter, then into cinnamon-sugar.

Press one apple slice into the top of each muffin.

Sprinkle lightly with cinnamon-sugar and bake for 25 minutes in the preheated oven, or until golden brown.

Quick Cheddar Bread

Categories: Breads, Cheese, Quickbreads

Servings: 4

Ingredient

- ❖ 3 3/4 c Unbleached Flour 5 ts Baking Powder
- ❖ 1/2 ts Salt 1/3 c Butter
- ❖ 2 1/2 c Cheddar; Sharp 1 1/2 c Milk
- ❖ 2 Eggs; Lg, Slightly Beaten

Preparation

Combine the dry ingredients, then cut butter into the flour until the mixture resembles coarse crumbs, then add cheddar cheese.

Combine the milk and eggs then add mixture to cheddar mixture.

Stir until just moistened, then spoon into a greased 9 X 5-inch loaf pan. Bake at 375 degrees F. hour.

Remove from the pan immediately and let cool on a wire rack.

Cheesy Corn Bread

Categories: Breads, Cheese, Quickbreads

Servings: 6

Ingredient

- ❖ 1 c Unbleached Flour 1 c Corn Meal; White Or Yellow
- ❖ 2 tb Sugar 1 tb Baking Powder
- ❖ 1 ts Salt 1/4 ts Mustard; Dry
- ❖ 2 c Cheddar; Sharp, Shredded 1 Egg; Lg, Slightly Beaten
- ❖ 1 c Milk 1/4 c Vegetable Oil

Preparation

Combine dry ingredients, then stir in the cheddar cheese.

Combine egg with the milk and oil. Stir into the cheddar mixture, mixing until just moistened.

Pour the mixture into a greased 9-inch square baking pan.

Bake at 425 degrees F. for 20 minutes. Cool slightly and cut into squares, then serve warm.

Cheddar Squares

Categories: Breads, Cheese, Quickbreads, Vegetables

Servings: 6

Ingredient

- ❖ 2 c Unbleached Flour 1 tb Baking Powder
- ❖ 1 ts Salt 1/3 c Butter
- ❖ 1 c Cheddar; Sharp, Shredded 1/2 c Onion; Chopped
- ❖ 2 tb Pimento; Chopped 2/3 c Milk

Preparation

Combine dry ingredients, then cut butter into the dry mixture until it resembles coarse crumbs.

Add the cheddar, onion, and pimento, mixing well. Add the milk, mixing until just moistened.

Spread the dough in a 9-inch square baking pan and bake at 450 degrees F. for 25 to 30 minutes or until a wooden pick inserted in the centre comes out clean.

Cool slightly and cut into squares. Serve warm.

Cheddar Date Nut Loaf

Categories: Breads, Cheese, Fruits, Quickbreads

Servings: 4

Ingredient

- ❖ 8 oz Dates; Finely Chopped 2 tb Butter
- ❖ 3/4 c Water; Boiling 1 3/4 c Unbleached Flour; Sifted
- ❖ 1/4 ts Salt 1 ts Baking Soda
- ❖ 1/2 c Sugar; Granulated 1 Egg; Lg, Well Beaten
- ❖ 4 oz Cheddar Md, Shredded 1 c Walnuts; Chopped

Preparation

Preheat the oven to 325 degrees F. Place the dates and butter in a small bowl and pour the boiling water over them.

Let stand for 5 minutes. Stir the dry ingredients together in a large bowl. Add the date mixture, egg, cheddar and nuts.

Mix until just blended and spoon the mixture into a well-greased 9 X 5-inch loaf pan. Let stand for 20 minutes. Bake for 50 to 60 minutes in the preheated oven or until a wooden pick inserted in the centre of the loaf comes out clean. Turn out onto a rack and cool before slicing.

NOTE: The flavour improves is the bread stands overnight before serving.

No-Knead Cheddar Rolls

Categories: Breads, Cheese, Yeast bread

Servings: 8

Ingredient

- ❖ 1 1/2 c Unbleached Flour; Unsifted 1 pk Active Dry Yeast; OR
- ❖ 1 tb Active Dry Yeast; Bulk 3 tb Sugar
- ❖ 1 ts Salt 3/4 c Milk
- ❖ 1/2 c Water 3 tb Butter
- ❖ 1 c Unbleached Flour; Unsifted 1 c Cheddar; Sharp, Grated
- ❖ 1/4 c Butter 1 Egg Yolk; Lg
- ❖ 1 tb Milk

Preparation

Place the grated cheese in a small bowl and cover to prevent drying then set aside.

Combine 1 1/2 cups unshifted flour, yeast, sugar, and salt in a large mixer bowl, blending thoroughly.

Measure 3/4 c of milk, water, and butter into a saucepan and heat until the liquids are warm, 115 to 120 degrees F.

Gradually add the liquids to the dry ingredients in the mixer bowl beating for 2 minutes at medium speed of electric mixer, scraping the bowl occasionally.

Add and beat in one cup of unshifted flour at high speed. Beat for 2 minutes, scraping the bowl occasionally. Mix in enough additional flour (1/2 to 1 cup unshifted) to make a soft dough.

(Dough will be slightly sticky.)

Put the dough into a greased deep bowl. Cover with waxed paper and a clean towel and let stand in a warm place until the dough has doubled, 45 to 60 minutes. Generously grease several baking sheets.

Melt the butter and set aside. Punch the dough down wit a fist and turn the dough out onto a lightly floured surface. Divide the dough into two equal portions. Set one portion aside. Roll the dough into a rectangle 16 X 8-inches.

Brush with about one-half of the melted butter. Sprinkle with about one half of the grated cheddar cheese.

Cut crosswise into 8 equal portions. Cut into halves lengthwise. Fold each strip into thirds, lapping each side portion over centre third. Place the rolls on a baking sheet. Repeat for the other half of the dough. Beat the egg yolk with the tbls of milk, slightly.

Brush the tops of the rolls with the egg yolk mixture. Let rise until doubled, about 30 minutes. Bake at 425 degrees F. for about 8 minutes or until rolls are golden brown. Serve rolls hot.

Panhandle Cornbread

Categories: Breads, Cheese, Quickbreads, Vegetables

Servings: 4

Ingredient

- ❖ 1 c Corn Meal; Yellow 1 tb Baking Powder
- ❖ 1 c Cheddar; Sharp, Shredded 2 Eggs; Lg, Beaten
- ❖ 1/2 c Vegetable Oil 1 c Dairy Sour Cream
- ❖ 8 oz Corn; Cream Style, 1 Cn 4 oz Green Chile Peppers; Chopped

Preparation

Preheat the oven to 400 degrees F. and generously grease a 12 cup bundt or 9-inch tube pan; set aside.

In a large bowl, combine the cornmeal and baking powder. Stir in the cheddar. In a medium bowl, beat the eggs, oil, sour cream, corn and chiles together. Add to the cornmeal mixture.

Stir until just moistened and then spoon the batter into the prepared pan. Bake for 40 to 50 minutes in the preheated oven until a wooden pick inserted in the centre comes out clean.

Cool on a rack for 10 minutes then invert over a serving plate.

Hearthside Cheddar Bread

Categories: Breads, Cheese, Fruits, Quickbreads

Servings: 4

Ingredient

- ❖ 2 1/2 c Unbleached Flour 1/2 c Sugar
- ❖ 2 ts Baking Powder 1 ts Salt
- ❖ 1/2 ts Cinnamon; Ground 3/4 c Milk
- ❖ 1/4 c Vegetable Oil 2 Eggs; Lg
- ❖ 1 1/2 c Apples; Cooking, * 2 c Cheddar; Sharp, Shredded
- ❖ 3/4 c Walnuts Or Pecans; Chopped

* Apples should be the cooking type (sour not sweet eating apples). They should be peeled, cored, and chopped.

Preparation

Preheat oven to 350 degrees F. and grease and flour a 9 X 5-inch loaf pan.

In a large bowl, combine the flour, sugar, baking powder, salt and cinnamon.

Make a well in centre of dry ingredients and add the milk, oil, and eggs. Stir until thoroughly combined.

Gently stir in the chopped apples, cheddar cheese, and nuts.

Bake for 1 hour and 15 minutes in the preheated oven until loaf is browned and sounds hollow when tapped on the bottom.

Cool in the pan on a rack for 5 minutes. Remove from the pan and cool to room temperature, on a wire rack, before slicing.

Sunrise Popovers

Categories: Breads, Cheese, Quickbreads

Servings: 8

Ingredient

- ❖ 4 tb Vegetable Shortening 1 1/3 c Unbleached Flour
- ❖ 1/2 ts Salt 2/3 c Milk
- ❖ 2/3 c Water 4 Eggs; Lg
- ❖ 1/2 c Cheddar; Sharp, Shredded

Preparation

Preheat the oven to 375 degrees F. Place eight 6-oz custard cups on a large baking sheet. Spoon 1 1/2 tsp of shortening into the bottom of each custard cup and set aside. Combine flour and salt in a large bowl, then gradually stir in the milk and water until well blended.

Beat in eggs, 1 at a time, beating until smooth after each addition. Fold in the cheddar cheese. Place baking sheet with custard cups in preheated oven for 3 to 5 minutes until the shortening melts and the custard cups are hot.

Fill custard cups ½ to 2/3rds full of batter. Bake for 45 minutes in preheated oven, without opening oven door until the popovers rise and turn golden brown. If not golden brown after 45 minutes, bake for an additional 5 minutes. Serve piping hot.

Polka Dot Quick Bread

Categories: Breads, Cheese, Quickbreads, Fruits

Servings: 4

Ingredient

- ❖ 2 c Cranberries; Fresh Or Frozen 1 c Milk
- ❖ 1 Egg; Lg, Slightly Beaten 1/4 c Butter; Melted
- ❖ 1 tb Orange Peel; Grated 2 c Unbleached Flour
- ❖ 1 c Sugar 1 tb Baking Powder
- ❖ 1/2 ts Salt 1 1/2 c Cheddar; Md, Shredded
- ❖ 1/2 c Walnuts; Coarsely Chopped

Preparation

Preheat oven to 350 degrees F. then grease a 9 X 5-inch loaf pan; set aside. Cut the cranberries in half and set aside in a small bowl.

In a medium bowl, combine the milk, egg, butter, and orange pee and set aside.

Sift the flour, sugar, baking powder, and salt into a large bowl. Ad the halved cranberries, cheese and nuts.

Toss with a fork to distribute. Add the milk mixture all at once an stir the flour mixture until just moistened.

Turn into the prepared loaf pan and bake for 1 hour and 15 minutes in the preheated oven or until a wooden pick inserted in the centre comes out clean.

Cool in pan on a rack for 10 minutes, then remove from the pan. Cool to room temperature on the wire rack before slicing.

Cheddar Braids

Categories: Breads, Cheese, Yeast bread

Servings: 8

Ingredient

- ❖ 1 c Water; Warm, 110-115 Deg. F. 1 pk Active Dry Yeast; OR
- ❖ 1 tb Active Dry Yeast; Bulk 3 1/2 c Unbleached Flour; *
- ❖ 1 ts Sugar 1 1/2 ts Salt
- ❖ 3/4 c Butter; Room Temperature 4 Eggs; Lg, Room Temperature
- ❖ 6 oz Cheddar; Extra Sharp, Diced 1 Egg; Lg
- ❖ 1 tb Milk 2 tb Celery Seeds

* You can use up to 4 1/2 cups of flour in this recipe depending on the weather.

Preparation

Pour the warm water into a warm bowl and add the yeast. Stir to dissolve then let stand until light and puffed, about 5 minutes. Add 1 1/2 cups of the flour, sugar and salt. Beat with an electric mixer on lowest speed for 1 minute. Beat on medium speed for 2 minutes longer. Add butter to yeast mixture and beat for another 1 minute

On the lowest speed on mixer, beat in 1 egg and ½ cup of flour until well blended, repeating until the 4 eggs are used up and enough flour has been added to make a soft sticky dough.

Continue to beat with mixer or by hand, until dough is glossy and elastic and pulls away from the side of the bowl. Stir in the cheddar cheese by hand. Cover and let rise in a warm place free from drafts until doubled in bulk, about 2 1/2 to 3 hours. When the dough has doubled in bulk, punch down and place in refrigerator for at least 5 hours or better, overnight.

Remove the dough from the refrigerator. Divide in half and cover and refrigerate the second ball of dough. Knead the remaining ball of dough on a lightly floured surface until soft and pliable.

Divide the dough into 3 equal parts and roll each piece into a rope 12 to 16-inches long. Braid the ropes, starting in the middle and working toward each end. Pinch the ends together so seal them.

Grease a large baking sheet and place the finished braid on one side of the sheet.

Repeat with the refrigerated dough. In a small bowl beat the egg and milk together. Brush braids with the egg mixture and let braids rise in a warm place, free from drafts, until dough in bulk, about 1 ½ to 2 hours. Do not cover.

Midway through the rising time, brush with the egg mixture again.

Preheat the oven to 400 degrees F.

When fully risen, brush with the egg mixture for a final time and sprinkle evenly with the celery seeds.

Bake for 40 minutes in the preheated oven until a wooden skewer or pick inserted in the braid comes out dry.

Remove from the oven and from the baking sheet. Cool to room temperature, on wire racks, before slicing.

Crusty Cheddar Bread

Categories: Breads, Cheese, Yeast bread

Servings: 4

Ingredient

- ❖ 1 pk Active Dry Yeast; OR 1 tb Active Dry Yeast; Bulk
- ❖ 1/4 c Water; Warm, 110-115 Deg. F. 1 c Cottage Cheese;
- ❖ 1 tb Sugar 1 1/4 ts Salt
- ❖ 1 Egg; Lg. 2 1/4 c Unbleached Flour; Unsifted,*
- ❖ 1 tb Butter; Room Temperature 1 c Cheddar; Sharp, grate

* The cottage cheese should be the small curd kind at room
temperature. **

You can use up to an extra 1/4 cup of flour in this recipe dependin
on the weather.

Preparation

Sprinkle the yeast over the warm water and let stand 5 minute
Gently stir to completely dissolve.

With an electric mixer, blend the softened yeast into cottage chees
sugar, salt and egg.

Add the flour in ½ cup portions to form a stiff but light dough and let rise in a warm place until doubled in bulk.

Butter a 1 ½ quart casserole dish and stir the dough down, then add 1 cup of the grated cheddar cheese. Turn into the buttered dish.

Let rise 30 to 40 minutes longer or until almost doubled in size.

Preheat oven to 350 degrees F. and bake for 40 to 50 minutes or until golden brown. Brush the top with butter.

Sourdough Starter #1

Categories: Breads

Servings: 1

Ingredient

- ❖ 2 c Unbleached Flour 1 pk Active Dry Yeast
- ❖ Water To Make Thick Batter

Preparation

Mix Flour with yeast. Add enough water to make a thick batter.

Set in warm place for 24 hours or until house is filled with a delectable yeasty smell.

Sourdough Starter #2

Categories: Breads

Servings: 1

Ingredient

❖ 2 c Unbleached Flour Water To Make Thick Batter

Preparation

Mix flour and water to make a thick batter. Let stand uncovered for four or five days, or until it begins working.

This basic recipe requires a carefully scalded container.

Sourdough Starter #3

Categories: Breads

Servings: 1

Ingredient

❖ 2 c Unbleached Flour Warm Milk to Make Thick Bat

Preparation

This starter is the same as starter #2 but uses warm Milk instead of water.

Use the same instructions.

Sourdough Starter #4

Categories: Breads

Servings: 1

Ingredient

❖ Unbleached Flour Potato Water

Preparation

Boil some potatoes for supper, save potato water, and use it lukewarm with enough unbleached flour to make a thick batter, without yeast.

This is a good way to make it in camp, where you have no yeast available and want fast results.

This is also the way most farm girls made it in the olden days. Let stand a day or so, or until it smells right.

Sourdough Starter #5

Categories: Breads

Servings: 1

Ingredient

- ❖ 4 c Unbleached Flour 2 tb Salt
- ❖ 2 tb Sugar 4 c Lukewarm Potato Water

Preparation

Put all ingredients in a crock or large jar and let stand in a warm place uncovered several days.

This is the authors last choice for making a starter but seems to be in all the cookbooks dealing with Sourdough Starters.

Use only as a last resort.

Sourdough Starter #6

Categories: Breads

Servings: 1

Ingredient

❖ 1 c Milk 1 c Unbleached Flour

Preparation

Let milk stand for a day or so in an uncovered container at room temperature.

Add flour to milk and let stand for another couple of days.

When it starts working well and smells right, it is ready to use.

NOTE: All containers for starters not using yeast, must be carefully scalded before use. If you are carless or do not scald them the starter will fail.

Sourdough Pancakes #1

Categories: Breads

Servings: 4

Ingredient

- ❖ 1 c Buttermilk Pancake Mix 1/2 c Active Starter
- ❖ 1/2 c Milk 1 Large Egg
- ❖ 1 tb Cooking Oil 1/2 ts Baking Powder

Preparation

Mix well and let stand a few moments.

Drop by large spoonsful on hot griddle.

NOTE: Berries of all kinds can be added to these recipes.

Sourdough Pancakes #2

Categories: Breads

Servings: 6

Ingredient

- ❖ 3 Large Eggs, Well Beaten 1 c Sweet Milk
- ❖ 2 c Active Starter 1 3/4 c Unbleached Flour
- ❖ 1 ts Baking Soda 2 ts Baking Powder
- ❖ 1 1/2 ts Salt 1/4 c Sugar

Preparation

Beat eggs. Add milk and starter. Sift together the flour, soda, baking powder, salt, and sugar.

Mix together. Drop onto hot griddle by large spoonsful.

NOTE: If ungreased griddle is used add 1/4 c Melted Fat to above recipe. Bacon fats give a great taste.

Sourdough French Bread

Categories: Breads

Servings: 18

Ingredient

- ❖ 1 pk Active Dry Yeast 1/4 c Warm Water (110 to 115 F)
- ❖ 4 1/2 c Unbleached Flour, Unsifted 2 tb sugar
- ❖ 2 ts Salt 1 c Warm Water
- ❖ 1/2 c Milk 2 tb Vegetable Oil
- ❖ 1/4 c Sourdough Starter

Preparation

Dissolve yeast in warm water. Add the rest of the ingredients. Mix and knead lightly and return to the bowl to rise until double.

Turn out onto floured board and divide dough into two parts.

Shape dough parts into oblongs and then roll them up tightly, beginning with one side.

Seal the outside edge by pinching and shape into size wanted. Place loaves on greased baking sheet and let rise until double again.

Make diagonal cuts on top of loaves with razor blade or VERY SHARP knife and brush lightly water for crisp crust.

Bake at 400 degrees F for about 25 minutes, or until brown and done.

NOTE: Makes 2 loaves at 18 slices each. Also note the serving size in all of these recipes is guesstimate. It all depends on the serving size you select.

The Doctor's Sourdough Bread

Categories: Breads

Servings: 18

Ingredient

- ❖ 1 c Sourdough Starter 2 c Warm Water
- ❖ 2 c Warm Milk 1 tb Butter
- ❖ 1 pk Active Dry Yeast 1/4 c Honey
- ❖ 7 c Unbleached Flour 1/4 c Wheat Germ
- ❖ 2 tb Sugar 2 ts Salt
- ❖ 2 ts Baking Soda

Preparation

Mix the starter and 2 1/2 Cups of the flour and all the water night before you want to bake.

Let stand in warm place overnight. Next morning mix in the butter with warm milk and stir in yeast until dissolved.

Add honey and when thoroughly mixed, add 2 more cups of flour, and stir in the wheat germ.

Sprinkle sugar, salt, and baking soda over the mixture.

Gently press into dough and mix lightly. Allow to stand from 30 to 50 minutes until mixture is bubbly.

Add enough flour until the dough cleans the sides of the bowl. Then place the dough on a lightly floured board and lead 100 times or until silky mixture is developed.

Form into 4 1-lb loaves, place in well-greased loaf pans 9 x 3 size.

Let rise until double, about 2 to 3 hours in a warm room. Then bake in hot oven, 400 degrees F, for 20 minutes.

Reduce oven temperature to 325 degrees F. and bake 20 minutes longer or until thoroughly baked.

Remove from pans and place loaves on rack to cool. Butter tops of loaves to prevent hard crustiness. Makes 4 1-lb Loaves.

Honeymoon Sourdoughs

Categories: Breads

Servings: 4

Ingredient

- ❖ 1 c Active Starter 1 1/4 c Prepared Biscuit Mix
- ❖ 1/2 ts Baking Powder 1 tb Cooking oil

Preparation

Mix all ingredients thoroughly and turn out onto a floured board, knead lightly and then roll out gently and cut into biscuits.

Brush lightly with melted butter or margarine.

Place of greased cookie sheet and bake at 450 degrees for about 1 minutes. Makes 9 Large biscuits.

Aunt Maria's Biscuits

Categories: Breads

Servings: 4

Ingredient

- ❖ 1 1/2 c Sifted Unbleached Flour 3 ts Baking Powder
- ❖ 1 ts Salt 1 1/2 ts Baking Soda *
- ❖ 2 tb Sugar 1/4 c Shortening, Melted
- ❖ 1 1/2 c Sourdough Starter

Preparation

* More Baking Soda may be added if the starter if very sour.

Place flour in bowl, add starter in a well, then add melted shortenin and dry ingredients.

Mix lightly and turn out onto a lightly floured board and knead unt the consistency of bread dough, or of a satiny finish.

Pat or roll out dough to 1/2-inch thickness, cut, put on a greased pan. Coat all sides of biscuits with melted butter.

Let rise over boiling water for 1/2 hour. Bake at 425 degrees F fc 15 to 20 minutes.

Anna's Sourdough Biscuits

Categories: Breads

Servings: 4

Ingredient

- ❖ 1/2 c Active Starter 1 c Milk
- ❖ 2 1/2 c Flour 1/3 c Lard or Shortening
- ❖ 1 tb Sugar 3/4 ts Salt
- ❖ 2 ts Baking Powder 1/2 ts Baking Soda
- ❖ 1/4 ts Cream Of Tartar

Preparation

At bedtime make a batter of the half cup of starter, cup of milk, an 1 cup of the flour. Let set overnight if the biscuits are wanted fo breakfast.

If wanted for noon, the batter maybe mixed in the morning and se in a warm place to rise. However, unless the weather is warm, it i always all right to let it ferment overnight. It will get very light an bubbly.

When ready to mix the biscuits, sift together the remaining cup an a half of flour and all other dry ingredients except the baking soda

Work in the lard or shortening with your fingers or a fork.

Add baking soda dissolved in a little warm water to the sponge and then add the flour mixture.

Mix into a soft dough. Knead lightly a few times to get in shape. Roll out to about 1/2-inch thickness or a little thicker and cut with a biscuit cutter.

Place close together in a 9 x 13-inch pan, turning to grease tops.

Cover and set in a warm place to rise for about 45 minutes. Bake in a 375-degree oven for about 30 to 35 minutes.

Leftovers are good split and toasted in a sandwich toaster.

Sheepherder Bread

Categories: Breads

Servings: 18

Ingredient

- ❖ 1 1/2 c Active Sourdough Starter 4 c Unbleached Flour
- ❖ 2 tb Sugar 2 tb Shortening, Melted
- ❖ 1 ts Salt 1/4 ts Baking Soda

Preparation

Into a large bowl, sift the dry ingredients, and dig a well in the centr of the sourdough starter.

Blend the dry mix into the starter from the edges with enough flou to knead until smooth and shiny.

Place in greased bowl and let rise until almost double. Shape into loaves and place in greased bread pans.

Bake at 375 degrees F until done.

Sourdough Sams

Categories: Breads

Servings: 4

Ingredient

- ❖ 1/2 c Active Sourdough Starter 1/2 c Sugar
- ❖ 2 tb Shortening 2 c Unbleached Flour
- ❖ 1 ts Baking Powder 1 Large Egg
- ❖ 1/2 ts Nutmeg 1/4 ts Cinnamon
- ❖ 1/2 ts Baking Soda 1/2 ts Salt
- ❖ 1/3 c Buttermilk or Sour Milk

Preparation

Sift dry ingredients, stir into liquid, roll out and cut with a regular donut cutter. Then heat some oil in a deep fryer to 390 degrees F and fry.

Makes about 17 Doughnuts with holes. Just before serving dust with powdered or cinnamon sugar.

NOTE: These doughnuts are virtually greaseless. And if you want you can make several batches at a time and freeze. They keep well and to me taste after a while in the freezer. Take out as many as needed and thaw and put sugar on or eat plain.

100% Whole Wheat Bread

Categories: Breads, Yeast

Servings: 6

Ingredient

- ❖ 2/3 c Water 3 pk Yeast
- ❖ 1 tb Sugar 8 c Scalded milk
- ❖ 2/3 c Shortening 1 c Sugar
- ❖ 1/2 c Molasses 2 tb Salt
- ❖ 12 c Whole wheat flour

Preparation

Dissolve yeast in 2/3 c water while your milk is cooling. Dissolve
cup sugar in the hot milk. Stir all ingredients in large bowl, turn ou
and knead about 5 minutes, adding flour if needed. Knead about
minutes. Let rise until doubled in bulk, about 1 1/2 to 2 hours.

Knead down and shape into 6 loaves, let rise until doubled in pans

Bake at 375 degrees F. For 40 minutes. Turn out on wire rack and
let cool to cold before slicing if you can.

NOTE: Raisins and/or walnuts can be added for a change. Also,
this bread freezes well.

Bacon, Cheese, And Tomato Sandwiches

Categories: Vegetables, Breads

Servings: 3

Ingredient

- ❖ 3 Slices bacon 3 Slices rye bread, toasted
- ❖ 2 tb Mayo. or salad dressing 1/2 ts Dried dill weed
- ❖ 1 Large tomato, sliced 3 Slices swiss cheese

Preparation

Place bacon on microwave rack in glass dish. Cover loosely and microwave until crisp, 2 1/2 to 3 1/2 minutes.

Spread toast with mayonnaise, sprinkle with dill.

Place toast slices on serving plate; top with tomato, cheese slices.

Crumble bacon and sprinkle over top.

Microwave uncovered on high (100%) until cheese begins to melt, 1 to 1 ½ minutes.

Corn Bread

Categories: Penndutch, Breads

Servings: 1

Ingredient

- ❖ 1 c Cornmeal, yellow *or:
- ❖ 1 c Cornmeal, white 4 tb Sugar
- ❖ 1 ts Salt 1 Egg, well beaten
- ❖ 1 c Milk, skim 1 c Flour
- ❖ 4 ts Baking powder 2 tb Butter, melted

Preparation

Add sugar and salt to the cornmeal. Beat the egg well and pour into the milk; stir this mixture into the meal, beating thoroughly.

Sift flour and baking powder into the meal, add melted butter and beat hard. Pour the mixture into a greased pan and bake at 400-F until brown.

To make a thin crisp Johnny Cake, use an oblong pan and spread batter thinly. For a soft loaf, spread batter thickly.

Source: Pennsylvania Dutch Cook Book - Fine Old Recipes, Culinary Arts Press, 1936.

Ham and Cheese with Coleslaw

Categories: Main dish, Vegetables, Breads

Servings: 4

Ingredient

- ❖ 2 tb Margarine or butter 1/2 ts Prepared mustard
- ❖ 4 Slices rye bread, toasted 4 Slices cooked ham
- ❖ 1 Large tomato, sliced 4 Slices cheese
- ❖ 1 c Coleslaw

Preparation

Microwave margarine uncovered in custard cup on high (100% until softened, 15 to 30 seconds. Blend in mustard.

Spread margarine on one side of each toast slice. Place slices buttered sides up on serving plate; top with the ham, tomato and cheese slices.

Microwave uncovered until cheese begins to melt, 1 1/2 to 2 minutes. Top each sandwich with a spoonful of coleslaw.

High-Protein Muffins

Categories: Muffins, Breads, Breakfast

Servings: 10

Ingredient

- ❖ 1 1/2 c Raisins 1 3/4 c Milk
- ❖ 1 c Stirred whole wheat flour 1 c Soy flour
- ❖ 1 c Toasted wheat germ 4 ts Baking powder
- ❖ 1 1/2 ts Ground nutmeg 3/4 ts Salt
- ❖ 4 Large eggs, slightly beaten 2/3 c Honey
- ❖ 2/3 c Vegetable oil 1/4 c Dark molasses

Preparation

Combine Bran Flakes, raisins, and milk in large mixing bowl.

Stir together whole wheat flour, soy flour, wheat germ, baking powder, nutmeg and salt; set aside. Combine eggs, honey, oil and molasses in small bowl; blend well.

Add egg mixture to soaked bran flakes; mix. Add dry ingredients all at once to bran mixture, stirring just enough to moisten.

Spoon batter into paper-lined 3-inch muffin-pan cups, filling 2/3rds full. Bake in 350 degrees F. oven 25 minutes or until golden brown. Serve hot with butter and homemade jelly or jam.

Nifty Hamburgers on A Bun

Categories: Breads, Hamburgers, Meats

Servings: 4

Ingredient

- ❖ 8 Hamburger buns; * Prepared mustard or catsup
- ❖ 1 lb Lean ground beef 1/4 c Onion; chopped, 1 small
- ❖ 1 ts Salt 1/4 ts Pepper

* Hamburger buns should be the small ones or use 6 slices of bread.

Preparation

Heat oven to 500 degrees F. Spread cut sides of hamburgers buns or one side of each bread slice with mustard. Mix meat, onion, salt and pepper.

Spread mixture over the mustard, being careful to bring it to the edges of the buns.

Place meat sides up on an ungreased baking sheet.

Bake until desired doneness is reached, about 5 minutes.

NOTE: If you like, you can have these burgers ready and waiting in the freezer for last-minute cooking.

After spreading the meat mixture over the buns, wrap each securely in heavy-duty or double thickness of regular aluminium foil and label; freeze no longer than 2 months.

To serve, unwrap desired number of hamburgers and bake about 10 minutes.

Apple Strudel (Apfelstrudel)

Categories: Penndutch, Breads, Fruits

Servings: 1

Ingredient

- ❖ 2 1/2 c Flour 1 ts Salt
- ❖ 2 tb Shortening 2 Egg, slightly beaten
- ❖ 1/2 c Water, warm 5 c Apple, sliced
- ❖ 1 c Brown sugar 1/2 c Raisins
- ❖ 1/2 c Nuts, chopped 3 tb Butter, melted
- ❖ 1/2 ts Cinnamon 1 Lemon, grated rind of

Preparation

Sift the flour and salt together. Cut in 2 Tbsp shortening and add the eggs and water. Knead well, then throw or beat dough against board until it blisters. Stand it in a warm place under a cloth for 20 minutes. Cover kitchen table with a small white cloth and flour it. Put dough on it. Pull out with hands very carefully to thickness of tissue paper. Spread with mixture made of sliced apples, melted butter, raisins, nuts, brown sugar, cinnamon and grated lemon rind. Fold in outer edges and roll about 4 inches wide. Bake at 450-F for 10 minutes, reduce heat to 400-F and continue to bake about 20 minutes. Let cool. Cut in slices about 2 inches wide.

Cinnamon Buns (The Famous Dutch Sticky Buns)

Categories: Penndutch, Breads

Servings: 1

Ingredient

- ❖ 1 c Milk, scalded 1/2 c Raisins, chopped
- ❖ 2 tb Currants 1/2 ts Cinnamon
- ❖ Brown sugar 2 tb Citron, finely chopped
- ❖ 1/2 c Yeast *dissolved in:
- ❖ 1/4 c Water, warm 3 c Flour
- ❖ 1/2 ts Salt 3 tb Butter

Preparation

Dissolve yeast in warm water; add to milk which has been allowed to become lukewarm. Add sugar (about 3 Tbsp), salt and flour, and knead thoroughly until it becomes a soft dough. Place the dough in a buttered bowl and butter the top of the dough.

Cover bowl and put in a warm place. Permit it to stand until dough becomes three times its original size.

Roll until it is one fourth of an inch in thickness, brush with butter and spread with raisins, currants, citron, brown sugar, cinnamon.

Roll as a jelly roll and cut into slices 3/4 inch thick. Place slices in buttered pans, spread well with brown sugar, and bake at 400-F for 20 minutes.